Sea Turtles

by Caroline Arnold
illustrated by Marshall Peck III

D0071789

SCHOLASTIC INC.
New York Toronto London Auckland Sydney

The setting sun glows red in the Florida sky. Insects swarm in the heavy summer air, and gentle waves splash the sand. Just beyond the surf, a large, dark shape looks toward the shore. It is a female loggerhead sea turtle. She is waiting for darkness. Then she will pull herself out of the water onto the beach. Along the shore, other turtles will join her. They will all dig holes and lay eggs. It is nesting time for sea turtles.

Five kinds of sea turtles live along the coasts of eastern North America. They are the loggerhead, hawksbill, Kemp's ridley, green, and leatherback turtles.

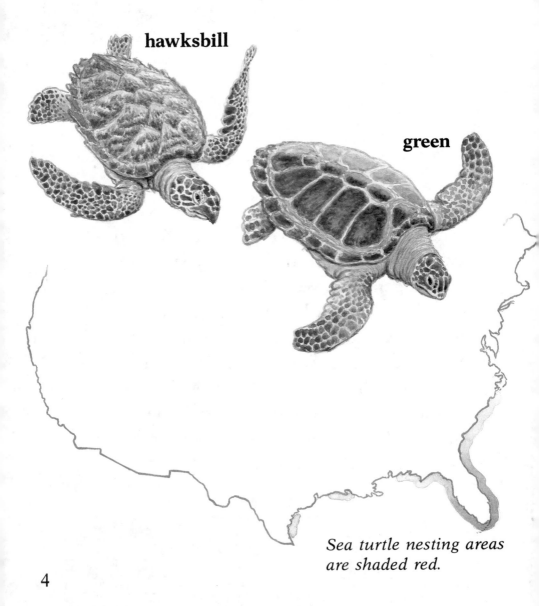

hawksbill

green

Sea turtle nesting areas are shaded red.

The loggerhead is the most common sea turtle in the United States. It has a thick, red-brown shell. It is named for its huge, log-like head. An adult loggerhead is about three-and-a-half feet (107 centimeters) long, and weighs up to 300 pounds (135 kilograms).

The coast of the southeastern United States is one of the world's main nesting areas for loggerhead sea turtles. More than 28,000 turtles nest there each year.

Kemp's ridley

loggerhead

leatherback

Turtles are reptiles. (Dinosaurs, snakes, lizards, and crocodiles are some other kinds of reptiles.) Reptiles have scaly skin. The tough scales help protect their bodies.

Almost all turtles have hard, bony shells. The top part of the shell is called the carapace (KAR-uh-pace). The bottom is called the plastron (PLAS-tron). The carapace and plastron are covered by large scales called scutes (SCOOTS).

The shell protects a turtle from the weather. It also helps the turtle defend itself against animals that want to harm it.

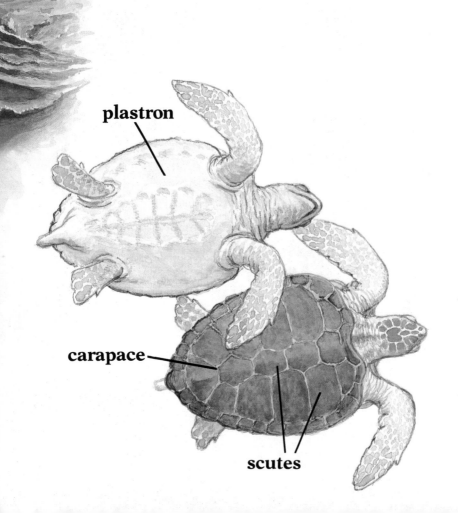

plastron

carapace

scutes

8

Loggerhead turtles usually feed in shallow water in bays and along coastlines. They mainly eat fish, crabs, and other small sea animals.

Turtles do not have teeth to chew their food. Instead, they use their sharp mouths to bite their food and then they swallow the pieces.

The broad, flat feet of a sea turtle are like flippers. The turtle uses them to push itself through the water. Sea turtles are strong swimmers. A loggerhead may swim 40 miles (64 kilometers) a day as it searches for food.

Turtles are graceful swimmers in the sea. But on land, they are clumsy and slow.

The only time sea turtles come to shore is during the nesting season. Most turtles nest in the spring and summer.

Sea turtles mate in the water. Only the female comes on land. She waits for night. Then she swims to the edge of the water. She smells the sand. If it smells familiar, she comes on shore. A female sea turtle almost always lays her eggs on the same beach. It is the beach where she hatched many years ago.

The female sea turtle uses her front
flippers to pull herself onto the beach.
Inch by inch she climbs up above the tide
line. Her trail looks like a row of tire
tracks in the sand.

The female loggerhead turtle begins to make her nest by scraping a layer of sand with her front flippers. This makes a shallow pit for her body. Then she uses her back feet to scoop out a hole. When the hole is about 18 inches (46 centimeters) deep and 12 inches (30 centimeters) wide, she stops. Then she lowers her tail and starts to lay her eggs.

One by one the eggs drop down in a neat pile. Each one is a little smaller than a Ping-Pong ball and has a white, leathery shell. Soon there are more than 100 eggs in the nest!

When a sea turtle is laying her eggs, she sometimes seems to cry. She is not sad. The tears are a way of getting rid of extra salt in her body.

This is the actual size of sea turtle eggs.

13

When the female sea turtle is finished laying her eggs, she takes a short rest. Then she uses her flippers to push sand back into the hole. When the hole is full, she stands over it. With a firm thud, she drops her body onto the sand. Again and again she falls. Her smooth plastron packs the sand. Then she uses her flippers to scatter loose sand across the top. Now her nest is finished. By the time dawn breaks, she will be swimming back out to sea.

A few weeks later, the female sea turtle may return to make another nest. She may make several nests in one season.

Most sea turtles do not lay eggs every season. Some nest every other year. Others nest once every three years or more.

The sun keeps the turtle eggs warm, and the water in the sand keeps them damp. Between six and nine weeks after they were laid, the eggs will be ready to hatch.

The length of time to hatching varies with the temperature and dampness of the nest. Scientists recently found out something else. When eggs of a loggerhead turtle are kept above 86 degrees Fahrenheit (30 degrees Celsius), most of the turtles inside grow to be females. When the eggs are kept below 86 degrees Fahrenheit (30 degrees Celsius), the turtles become males.

Nests made in the hottest months usually have more females. So do those in sunny places. Nests in the shade usually have more males.

wild hog

ghost crab

Not all turtle eggs hatch. Storms and high tides sometimes wash away nests that are too close to the shore. Animals such as raccoons, foxes, wild hogs, and ghost crabs also destroy turtle nests. They like to eat the eggs.

fox

raccoon

A yellow yolk inside each egg provides food for the growing turtle. By the time the turtle is ready to hatch, the yolk is used up.

The baby turtle has a sharp knob on its nose called an egg tooth. When it is ready to hatch, the turtle pushes its egg tooth against the shell and slits the shell open. Soon after hatching, the egg tooth falls off. The young turtle no longer needs it.

After its shell is broken, the turtle wiggles out. The movement of one turtle tells the turtles in nearby eggs to start hatching, too. Soon all the turtles are hatching at once. The turtles on the bottom of the nest step on the falling sand and make it firm. Finally the turtles on top pull down the roof of the nest. Then the baby turtles wait for night.

*The shell of a newly hatched loggerhead
is one-and-a-half inches (38 centimeters) long,
or a little bigger than a silver dollar.*

When it is dark, the newly hatched turtles scramble out of their hole and dash to the sea.

This is the most dangerous time in a sea turtle's life. A baby turtle makes a tasty meal for a raccoon, sea gull, or crab. The tiny turtles crawl as fast as they can across the sand and into the water.

The baby turtles know where to go even
when they cannot see the ocean. The sky
over the water is brighter than the sky
over the land. This helps the turtles find
their way to the sea. By instinct, turtles
head for the brighter sky.

If baby turtles see the lights of cars or
houses, they may go the wrong way. Every
year many turtles try to cross roads and
get hit by cars. Many beach communities
now tell people to turn off their lights
during the turtle-nesting season.

Life in the sea is dangerous for turtles, too. Fish and whales catch and eat turtles. Only a few baby turtles survive to be adults.

The newly hatched turtles float on top of the water. They paddle their feet to swim and drift with the ocean currents. Some of the turtles live in beds of floating seaweed. The seaweed helps the turtles hide from animals that want to eat them. The young turtles eat small fish, worms, and other food that they find in the seaweed.

When a loggerhead turtle is one year old, it is about six inches (15 centimeters) long. Sea turtles grow slowly. A female loggerhead may not be big enough to breed for the first time until she is 20 years old or more.

No one knows exactly how long sea turtles can live. Some may reach the age of 100 or more.

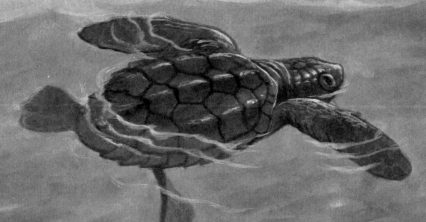

When winter comes, most sea turtles along the coast of North America swim to warmer water further south. They return the following spring.

How do the turtles find their way?

Sea turtles swim near the top of the water. They can see the sky. They may use the sun and stars as a map to show them the way. When the turtles get close to shore, they can see landmarks such as rocks and trees.

When we travel, we can use a compass to find our direction. The magnetic needle in the compass always points north. Scientists have found that sea turtles have small magnets in their brains. They use the magnets as built-in compasses.

The direction of the ocean waves also helps sea turtles know which way to swim. The turtles' sense of smell may guide them, too.

Every year fewer turtles come to shore to nest. In some places, nesting beaches are no longer used at all. Some kinds of sea turtles may soon become extinct.

Why are sea turtles in danger?

For many years people have killed sea turtles for their meat and shells. They also collect and eat turtle eggs. It is now against the law to do these things. But not everybody in the world obeys the law.

In some places, houses and roads are too close to turtle-nesting beaches. The lights and noise disturb the turtles and keep them from building nests.

Some turtles are injured by motor boats, or get caught in fishing nets and drown.

Pollution in the ocean also kills turtles.

Scientists are trying to learn more about sea turtles. Then we will know better how to help sea turtles and preserve the places where they live.

In many places, people are helping sea turtles. They watch turtles that come to shore and take care of any that are sick or injured. They check to make sure that turtles make their nests in safe places. Sometimes people put a wire fence over a nest to protect it. Or, they may move the eggs to a turtle hatchery. They try to help the young turtles get a good start in life. Then they will have a better chance for survival.

Sea turtles have been swimming in the oceans of the world for millions of years. They are reminders of what life was like long ago. Now their future depends on us.

Index

About the Author

Photo by Richard Hewett

Caroline Arnold is the author of more than eighty books for children, including award-winning titles such as *Koala*, *Saving the Peregrine Falcon*, and *Dinosaur Mountain*. When she was growing up in Minneapolis, Minnesota, she spent her summers at a camp in northern Wisconsin. That is where she first developed her interest in animals and the out-of-doors.

Today she goes to zoos, museums, and wildlife parks as part of the research for her books. Ms. Arnold lives in Los Angeles, California, with her husband, who is a neuroscientist, and their two children. Ms. Arnold also teaches part-time in the Writers' Program at UCLA Extension.

If You Want to Read More About Sea Turtles:

Loggerhead Turtle, by Jack Denton Scott (G.P. Putnam's Sons, 1974).
Scaly Babies, by Ginny Johnston and Judy Cutchins (Morrow Junior Books, 1988).
Turtle Watch, by George Ancona (Macmillan, 1987).
When Turtles Come to Town, by Cary B. Ziter (Franklin Watts, 1989).

Library of Congress Cataloging-in-Publication Data

Arnold, Caroline.
Sea turtles / by Caroline Arnold ; illustrated by Marshall Peck.
p.   cm.
ISBN 0-590-46945-2
1. Sea turtles — Juvenile literature. [1. Sea turtles. 2. Turtles.]
I. Peck, Marshall H., ill. II. Title.
QL666.C536A76   1994
597.92 — dc20
93-6353
CIP
AC

12 11 10 9 8 7 6 5 4 3 2   4 5 6 7 8 9/9

Printed in the U.S.A.   23

First Scholastic printing, April 1994

Book design by Laurie McBarnette